Pink Princess TEA PARTIES

Barbara Beery

Gibbs Smith, Publisher
TO ENRICH AND INSPIRE HUMANKIND
Salt Lake City | Charleston | Santa Fe | Santa Barbara

First Edition
12 11 10 09 08   15 14 13 12 11 10 9 8 7 6 5 4 3 2

Text © 2008 Barbara Beery
Photographs © 2008 Zachary Williams
Food styling by Joanne Voorhees

Published by
Gibbs Smith, Publisher
P.O. Box 667
Layton, Utah 84041

Orders: 1.800.835.4993
www.gibbs-smith.com
www.batterupkids.com
www.kidscookingshop.com
Designed by Dawn DeVries Sokol
Printed and bound in China

Library of Congress Cataloging-in-Publication Data
Beery, Barbara, 1954–
  Pink princess tea parties / Barbara Beery. — 1st ed.
     p. cm.
  ISBN-13: 978-1-4236-0416-7
  ISBN-10: 1-4236-0416-4
  1. Afternoon teas—Juvenile literature. 2. Children's parties—Juvenile literature.
  3. Cookery—Juvenile literature. I. Title.

TX736.B43 2008
641.5'3—dc22
                              2007049984

Contents

Tea Time Sippers

Sweet Chai Tea 4

Perfect Pink Lemonade 7

Frozen Peppermint Hot Chocolate 8

Sugar-and-Spice Cider 11

Pink Princess Smoothie 12

Homemade Cherry-Vanilla
Cream Soda 15

Enchanted Tutti-Frutti Tea 16

Tea Time Cookies and Cakes

Pastel Petits Fours 19

Teacup Cupcakes 20

Pink Princess Mini Cupcakes 23

Princess Cookies 24

Sweetheart Shortbread 27

Confetti Meringue Cookies 31

Ladybug Cookies 32

Tea Time Sweets and Treats

Royal Raspberry Tarts 35

Peanut Butter and Jelly Scones 36

Fairytale Chocolate Muffins 39

Fruit and Muffins en Brochette 40

Princess Candy Crunch 42

Cute as a Cream Puff 45

Dreamy Dipped Strawberries 46

Victorian Princess Ice Cream 49

Gingerbread Tea Loaves 50

Tea Time Sandwiches and Snacks

Little Lady Fruit Sandwiches 53

Bitsy Bacon and Cheese Rolls 54

Rainbow-Colored Eggs 57

Pink-and-White Star Bites 58

Jeweled Crown Biscuits 60

Fairy Princess Fruity Toast 61

Chicken Salad Sushi Rolls 63

Sweet Chai Tea

Let's start stirring!

4 cups filtered water

3 regular tea bags*

2 cinnamon sticks

6 cardamom seeds

3 whole cloves

6 black peppercorns

¼ teaspoon freshly grated nutmeg

½ inch thinly sliced fresh ginger

1 cup plain or vanilla soy milk

4 teaspoons honey or
    maple syrup

*English breakfast tea, orange
    pekoe, Darjeeling, or Earl Grey

Makes 4–5 servings

Place water, tea bags, and all spices in a large saucepan over medium heat and bring to a boil. Reduce heat and simmer 10 to 15 minutes.

Remove from heat and add soy milk. Return to heat and simmer another 5 minutes, or until steaming. Remove from heat.

Pour chai through a large strainer into a teapot. Stir in honey or maple syrup and serve. Or chai may be covered and refrigerated for up to 1 day and then served cold over crushed ice.

It's a sweet tea party!

Perfect Pink Lemonade

2 liters flavored sparkling
water (strawberry, raspberry,
or lemon), chilled

½ cup grenadine syrup

Juice of 8 to 10 lemons

½ cup sugar (or more to taste)

Crushed ice (optional)

Pink or purple sugar crystals
(optional)

Makes 15 servings

Let's get juicing!

Combine chilled flavored sparkling water,
grenadine, lemon juice, and sugar. Stir with
a metal whisk to blend ingredients. Add
crushed ice if desired.

If desired, moisten rim of small punch cups
or fancy juice glasses and dip in pink or
purple sugar crystals. Pour lemonade
immediately into cups or glasses and serve.

Picture-perfect sipping!

Frozen Peppermint Hot Chocolate

Frozen Peppermint Whipped Topping

1 (8-ounce) container frozen whipped topping, thawed

10 to 12 hard peppermint candies, crushed

1 to 2 drops red food coloring

Hot Chocolate

4 cups whole or reduced-fat milk

Pinch salt

1½ cups milk chocolate or semisweet chocolate chips

1 teaspoon vanilla extract

Makes 8 servings

A warm and frosty sweet delight!

Let's get freezing!

Line a cookie sheet with foil or waxed paper. Set aside.

In a large mixing bowl, combine half of the whipped topping with crushed peppermints. Add a drop or two of red food coloring and stir to blend.

Drop 8 teaspoonfuls of whipped topping in the shape of dollops, about 1½ to 2 inches in diameter, on the prepared cookie sheet. Place cookie sheet in the freezer and freeze until firm, about 20 to 30 minutes.

Heat milk and salt in a large saucepan over medium heat until steaming. Remove from heat and add chocolate chips. Return to low heat and whisk until chocolate chips are melted and mixture is smooth. Remove hot chocolate from heat and add vanilla.

Carefully ladle into teacups or small mugs. Garnish each drink with a dollop of frozen peppermint whipped topping.

Sugar-and-Spice Cider

1 gallon apple cider

3 cups pomegranate juice

4 cinnamon sticks

10 whole cloves

½ teaspoon vanilla extract

½ cup dried cranberries

1 orange, thinly sliced

Makes 15 servings

Let's start stirring!

In a large saucepan, combine apple cider, pomegranate juice, cinnamon sticks, and cloves. Heat over low heat until mixture begins to simmer. Remove from heat and add vanilla, dried cranberries, and orange slices.

Place saucepan back over low heat and stir until mixture begins to steam. Remove from heat and ladle into teacups or small glass punch cups.

Sugar and spice and everything nice!

Pink Princess Smoothie

Let's get whirling!

1½ cups orange juice

1 banana, sliced

1 cup frozen strawberries

1 cup frozen raspberries

½ teaspoon vanilla extract

Fresh strawberries or
raspberries for garnish

Makes 2 smoothies

Combine all ingredients except fruit for garnish in a blender and mix until smooth and creamy.

Pour into pretty glasses and garnish with fresh fruit as desired.

Fruit for a princess!

Homemade Cherry-Vanilla Cream Soda

Let's get fizzing!

2 cups sugar

1 cup water

1 tablespoon vanilla extract

3 to 5 cups crushed
   or cubed ice

4 liters sugar-free cherry-
   flavored sparkling water

1 (4-ounce) bottle maraschino
   cherries, with juice

1 cup half-and-half

Makes 24 servings

In a medium saucepan, combine sugar and water. Heat for about 5 minutes over medium heat, stirring with a wooden spoon until sugar has dissolved and liquid becomes clear.

Remove from heat and add vanilla. Set aside to cool for 10 minutes. (The cooked liquid is called simple syrup.) Transfer simple syrup to a container with a lid and put in the refrigerator to chill for at least 1 hour or up to 1 week.

To make the cream sodas, combine the simple syrup, ice, and sparkling water. Add maraschino cherries with juice. Pour into glasses and top each with a little half-and-half. Serve immediately.

Old-fashioned fun!

Enchanted Tutti-Frutti Tea

Let's get chilling!

1 lemon, sliced

1 orange, sliced

1 cup raspberries

1 peach, sliced and skin removed

6 bags raspberry or mango tea

6 cups boiling water

2 cups white grape juice

½ cup honey

Makes 10-12 servings

Freeze all fruits in a single layer on a cookie sheet for 1 hour or up to 1 day.

In a heatproof container, combine tea and boiling water. Steep 5 minutes and then remove tea bags with metal tongs. Discard bags.

Stir in grape juice and honey. Transfer to a container with a lid and chill for 1 to 2 hours.

When ready to serve, pour tea into a punch bowl, stir in frozen fruits, and serve.

A tutti-frutti treat!

Pastel Petits Fours

1 purchased family-size
 pound cake

9 cups powdered sugar

½ cup light corn syrup

½ to ¾ cup water

1 teaspoon vanilla extract

½ teaspoon almond extract

Pastel gel or paste food
 coloring

Sprinkles, fresh edible flowers,
 sugar crystal decorations

Makes about 16

Tiny treats
for tiny plates!

Let's cut the cake!

Trim about ¼ inch from each short end of the pound cake. Cut cake into 1-inch-thick slices. Use ½- to 1-inch cookie cutters of assorted shapes and cut 2 to 3 shapes from each slice of pound cake. Place cutout cakes on a wire rack set over a cookie sheet lined with foil. Set aside.

In a large saucepan, mix powdered sugar, corn syrup, ½ cup water, and vanilla and almond extracts together until warmed, smooth, and creamy. Remove saucepan from heat and cool icing for about 5 minutes in pan. Add the remaining ¼ cup water if needed to create a smooth, flowing icing. Divide icing equally between 2 to 3 small bowls and stir enough food coloring into each one to reach desired color.

Spoon icing over each little cake and decorate with assorted fancy toppings. Let stand uncovered at room temperature for about 30 minutes or until dry. Store in airtight container up to 3 days.

Teacup Cupcakes

Cupcakes

2 tablespoons cocoa powder

1 box chocolate cake mix

Milk

1 teaspoon vanilla extract

Frosting

2 cups butter, room temperature

2 cups powdered sugar

Food coloring

½ teaspoon vanilla extract

1 (16-ounce) jar marshmallow crème

Assorted candies or sprinkles

Makes 24 cupcakes

It's your "cup of tea!"

Let's get baking!

Preheat oven to 350 degrees F. Generously spray 24 heatproof teacups or muffin cup liners with nonstick cooking spray and dust with cocoa powder. Place on cookie sheets and set aside.

Make cupcake batter according to package directions, substituting milk for water and adding vanilla. Divide batter evenly between prepared teacups or muffin cup liners. Bake cupcakes according to package directions. Remove from oven and cool for 20 minutes.

In a large mixing bowl, beat the butter until creamy. Beat in half of the powdered sugar. Add the remaining powdered sugar and mix until light and fluffy. Add food coloring. Add vanilla and stir in the marshmallow crème until well blended.

Frost cupcakes and decorate teacups. Garnish with candies, sprinkles, and frosting rosettes.

Pink Princess Mini Cupcakes

Let's get baking!

Cupcakes

1 box strawberry cake mix

Cranberry juice

1 teaspoon vanilla extract

½ teaspoon strawberry extract

Sliced strawberries

Mint sprigs

48 pink oven-safe paper
   soufflé or nut cups*

Frosting

1 container purchased creamy
   vanilla frosting

2 cups powdered sugar

Pink paste food coloring

Do not use plastic cups.

Preheat oven to 350 degrees F. Make cup-cake batter according to package directions, substituting cranberry juice for water and adding vanilla and strawberry extracts.

Place 48 pink paper oven-safe soufflé or nut cups on a cookie sheet. Spray with nonstick cooking spray. Divide batter evenly between cups.

Bake cupcakes 10 to 12 minutes. Remove from oven and cool for 15 minutes before frosting.

Combine vanilla frosting, powdered sugar, and several dots of pink paste food coloring in a large bowl. Blend with an electric mixer until creamy.

Generously frost each cooled mini cupcake. Top with a strawberry slice and mint sprig.

Sweet strawberry bites!

Makes 48 mini cupcakes

Princess Cookies

Cookies

½ cup butter, room
   temperature

½ cup sugar

1 egg

½ teaspoon vanilla extract

2 cups flour

½ teaspoon baking soda

½ teaspoon salt

36 Popsicle or craft sticks

Let's make cookies!

Preheat oven to 375 degrees F. Line two
cookie sheets with foil and spray with nonstick cooking spray.

Cream butter in a large mixing bowl and
add sugar, beating until light and fluffy.
Add egg and vanilla, mixing well.

Stir flour, baking soda, and salt into
creamed mixture, blending well. Dough
will be very stiff.

Divide dough into thirds and roll each
portion to ½ inch thickness on a surface
lightly dusted with powdered sugar. Dip
cookie cutters in a small amount of
powdered sugar and cut out assorted shapes
from dough.

Insert a Popsicle or craft stick about 1 inch
into each cookie. Carefully place cookies 3
inches apart on prepared cookie sheets.

Frosting

3 tablespoons commercial
   meringue powder

2 cups powdered sugar

¼ cup warm water, plus 1 to 2
   tablespoons more if needed

1 teaspoon vanilla extract

½ teaspoon almond extract

Assorted food coloring

Candies and sprinkles

Makes 36 cookies

Bake for 10 to 12 minutes, or until lightly browned. Remove from oven to wire racks and cool 10 minutes before frosting.

To make frosting, combine meringue powder, powdered sugar, water, and vanilla and almond extracts in a mixing bowl. Beat on high speed with an electric mixer for 5 minutes.

Divide frosting into separate bowls and add food coloring as desired. Frost cooled cookies and decorate with assorted candies.

A cookie on a stick is a very clever trick!

Sweetheart Shortbread

½ cup butter, room
   temperature

¾ cup powdered sugar, divided

½ teaspoon almond extract

Pinch salt

¼ teaspoon cinnamon

1½ cups flour

Makes 12 to 14
little hearts

Mix it up!

Preheat oven to 325 degrees F. Line a cookie sheet with foil and spray with nonstick cooking spray.

In a large mixing bowl, combine the butter, ¼ cup powdered sugar, and almond extract with an electric mixer until light and fluffy. Add the salt and cinnamon. Slowly add the flour, ¼ cup at a time, mixing well after each addition.

As the batter thickens, stop using the mixer and use your hands to knead the mixture into a dough ball in the bowl.

Remove the dough ball from the bowl and knead it a few more times on a lightly floured surface. Use your hands or a rolling pin to flatten the dough in the shape of a large circle about ¼ inch thick.

Cut out shapes with a 1½-inch heart-shaped cookie cutter and place on prepared cookie sheet. Bake for 12 to 15 minutes, or until barely browned. Remove from oven and cool for 10 minutes before dusting with remaining powdered sugar. Store in an airtight container.

You're my sweetheart!

Confetti Meringue Cookies

3 egg whites, room temperature

¾ cup sugar

¼ teaspoon cream of tartar

¼ teaspoon vanilla or
   almond extract

½ cup confetti sprinkles,
   divided

Makes 18 to 24 cookies

Let's get mixing!

Preheat oven to 250 degrees F. Line two cookie sheets with foil.

In a large bowl, whip egg whites with a mixer until soft peaks form. With mixer running, slowly add sugar, 1 tablespoon at a time. Add cream of tartar and vanilla or almond extract. Continue beating until stiff peaks form. Fold in ¼ cup confetti sprinkles.

Spoon mounds (about 2 tablespoons each) about ½ inch apart onto prepared cookie sheets. Sprinkle each one evenly with the remaining confetti sprinkles.

Place both cookie sheets on the middle rack of the oven and bake for 1 hour. Turn off oven and leave oven door closed for another 10 minutes. Remove cookies from oven. Cool on cookie sheets for 10 minutes, then store in an airtight container until ready to serve.

Perfect for a party!

Ladybug Cookies

Let's make ladybugs!

24 vanilla wafer cookies

1 container purchased creamy
vanilla frosting

Red paste food coloring

½ cup chocolate chip mini
morsels

24 Milk Duds or Junior Mints

Makes 24 little ladybugs

Place cookies on a large cookie sheet that
has been lined with foil. Place the frosting
in a small bowl and add red paste food
coloring. Mix well.

Spread about ½ teaspoon of frosting on the
rounded side of each vanilla wafer.

Position 5 to 7 mini morsels on the top of
each frosted cookie to create the ladybug's
spots. Place a small amount of frosting on a
Milk Dud or Junior Mint and secure it to
a frosted cookie at the top edge to make
the ladybug's head. Repeat for all cookies.

Place entire cookie sheet with decorated
cookies in the refrigerator and chill for
10 minutes, or until ready to serve.

Tiny little ladybugs!

Royal Raspberry Tarts

Let's get rolling!

1 sheet puff pastry, slightly thawed

½ cup raspberry jam

1½ pints fresh raspberries

1 (6-ounce) container raspberry or vanilla yogurt

Makes 12-14 tarts

Fit for a queen!

Preheat oven to 425 degrees F. Line a cookie sheet with foil and spray with nonstick cooking spray.

Place pastry sheet on a lightly floured surface. With a rolling pin, smooth away creases. Using a 1-inch square cookie cutter, cut out pieces of puff pastry. Place squares on prepared cookie sheet ½ inch apart. Prick the center of each pastry with a fork to prevent puffing up too much while baking.

Bake for 15 minutes, or until lightly browned and slightly puffed. Remove from oven and cool on a wire rack for 10 minutes. Slice each tart in half lengthwise and set aside.

Slowly heat raspberry jam in a small saucepan, stirring until thinned, about 30 seconds.

Spread 2 teaspoons yogurt on bottom half of each pastry square. Top with a few raspberries, replace the pastry tops, and then drizzle with warm jam. Refrigerate until ready to serve.

Peanut Butter and Jelly Scones

Let's get mixing!

2 cups flour

½ cup brown sugar

2½ teaspoons baking powder

¼ teaspoon salt

¼ cup cold butter, cut into
    cubes

¾ cup creamy peanut butter

¼ cup milk

2 eggs, room temperature

2 teaspoons vanilla extract

1 cup jam, any kind

Makes 8–10 scones

Preheat oven to 375 degrees F. Line a
cookie sheet with foil and spray with
nonstick cooking spray.

In a large bowl, stir together the flour,
brown sugar, baking powder, and salt.
Sprinkle the butter cubes over the flour
mixture. With your fingers or using two
butter knives, cut in the butter until the
mixture resembles coarse crumbs.

Add the peanut butter, milk, eggs, and
vanilla and then stir to combine. Knead
with your hands until dough clumps
together. Remove dough from bowl and
place on a lightly floured surface. Pat the
dough into a ½ inch thickness.

Using a floured 2½- to 3-inch round biscuit
cutter, cut rounds from the dough. Put
a tablespoon of jam on 1 round and then
place another round of dough on top.
Gently press together and place on prepared

cookie sheet. Repeat until all scones are assembled.

Bake 15 to 20 minutes, or until lightly browned. Remove from oven and cool 5 minutes. Using a spatula, transfer the scones to a wire rack to cool. Serve warm or at room temperature.

The very best way for PB&J!!

Fairytale Chocolate Muffins

Let's mix it up!

1 cup milk chocolate chips

⅓ cup unsalted butter

¾ cup buttermilk

½ cup sugar

1 egg

2 teaspoons vanilla extract

1⅔ cups flour

1 teaspoon baking soda

½ teaspoon salt

1 cup white chocolate chips

Powdered sugar

Makes 12 muffins

Rich chocolaty
goodness!

Preheat the oven to 400 degrees F. Line a muffin tin with 12 paper liners and then place on a cookie sheet.

In a small saucepan, melt the milk chocolate chips with the butter over low heat. Remove from heat and cool 10 minutes.

Pour the chocolate-butter mixture into a large mixing bowl and add buttermilk, sugar, egg, and vanilla. Blend ingredients until smooth with a whisk.

With a spatula, stir in flour, baking soda, and salt. Fold in the white chocolate chips. Spoon the batter equally between the paper liners.

Bake for 20 to 25 minutes, or until the tops of muffins are puffed and slightly cracked. Remove muffin tin from oven and let stand at least 5 minutes before removing the muffins to cool on a wire rack. Dust with powdered sugar.

Fruit and Muffins en Brochette

Let's start baking!

Muffins

2 cups flour

½ cup sugar

3 teaspoons baking powder

½ teaspoon cinnamon

⅛ teaspoon salt

1 egg

¾ cup whole milk

⅓ cup vegetable oil

2 teaspoons vanilla extract

1 cup fresh blueberries

12 (6-inch) wooden skewers

Fruit for skewer*

1 cup fresh strawberries, halved

½ cup fresh raspberries or
   blackberries

Preheat oven to 400 degrees F. Spray a mini muffin tin with nonstick cooking spray and then place on a cookie sheet.

In a large mixing bowl, combine all dry ingredients and whisk until well blended. Add all remaining ingredients except blueberries and blend with a spatula to combine. Carefully fold in the fresh blueberries.

Spoon batter into prepared muffin tin and bake 10 to 15 minutes, or until muffins are golden brown. Remove and cool on a wire rack for 5 minutes.

Thread fruits and 2 to 3 mini muffins alternately on wooden skewers.

*Or use your favorite fruits in any combination.

The perfect breakfast on a stick!

1 cup grapes

1 cup melon balls

½ cup apple slices

Makes 24 mini muffins
and 12 skewers

Princess Candy Crunch

1 pound vanilla candy
   coating*

½ cup dried cranberries or
   cherries

½ cup golden raisins

Pink decorating sugar

Makes 8–10 servings

Crunchy candy
delight!

Let's get melting!

Line a cookie sheet with foil and spray with
nonstick cooking spray.

Melt candy coating according to package
directions. Carefully pour into a large bowl.

Add dried fruit and mix to combine. Pour
onto prepared cookie sheet. Gently shake
cookie sheet to distribute evenly. Sprinkle
with pink decorating sugar.

Place the cookie sheet in the refrigerator.
Chill 15 to 20 minutes to harden.
Remove from refrigerator and break
candy into pieces. Store in refrigerator
until ready to serve.

This is sometimes called vanilla almond bark.

Cute as a Cream Puff

1 package purchased frozen
   mini cream puffs

½ (8-ounce) container frozen
   whipped topping, thawed

1 tablespoon grenadine syrup
   or maraschino cherry juice

½ teaspoon vanilla extract

Powdered sugar

Makes 12 cream puffs

Let's get baking!

Place 12 cream puffs evenly apart on a
cookie sheet to thaw.

Place the whipped topping in a mixing
bowl. Add grenadine or maraschino cherry
juice and vanilla. Stir to blend.

Carefully slice the very top off each cream
puff. Frost each cream puff with topping
and replace top. Dust lightly with powdered sugar.

Light and creamy tiny bites!

Dreamy Dipped Strawberries

Let's get dipping!

Assorted sprinkles, candies,
  chopped nuts, and shredded
  coconut

1 pound vanilla candy coating*

24 strawberries

Makes 24

Line a cookie sheet with foil. Place sprinkles and other toppings in individual small bowls.

Melt candy coating according to package directions. Set aside to cool for 5 minutes, and then pour into a mixing bowl.

Place a small wooden skewer ½ inch into the stem end of a strawberry. Carefully dip the strawberry into the melted candy coating. Roll strawberry in topping of choice. Place on the prepared cookie sheet and carefully remove skewer. Repeat until all strawberries are dipped and decorated.

Place cookie sheet in refrigerator for 10 minutes, or until ready to serve. Store any leftover strawberries in the refrigerator for up to 1 day.

This is sometimes called vanilla almond bark.

They're a dream!

Victorian Princess Ice Cream

Let's get chilling!

½ gallon Neapolitan ice cream

1 (8-ounce) bottle chocolate sauce

1 (10-ounce) bottle maraschino cherries, with stems

Makes 12 servings

Line a muffin tin with 12 paper liners.

Take ice cream from freezer and soften for about 10 minutes. Put 1 scoop of ice cream into each paper liner.

Carefully press ice cream into liner and smooth the tops of each ice cream cup. Place in the freezer for 1 hour, or until ready to serve.

When ready to serve, remove muffin tin from freezer and then peel the paper liner from each ice cream cup. Invert ice cream cups onto serving plates, drizzle with chocolate sauce, and garnish with a maraschino cherry.

You'll feel like a princess!

Gingerbread Tea Loaves

Let's get baking!

½ cup butter, room temperature

¾ cup packed light brown
   sugar

2 cups flour

1 teaspoon baking soda

2 teaspoons ground ginger

1 teaspoon ground cinnamon

¼ teaspoon ground cloves

½ teaspoon salt

2 eggs

½ cup molasses

⅔ cup apple juice

Makes 10-12 servings

Preheat oven to 350 degrees F. Line a
9-inch baking pan with foil that extends
1 inch past two ends of the pan. Spray foil
with nonstick cooking spray.

In a large bowl, combine butter and brown
sugar. Blend with a mixer on medium-high
speed until fluffy, about 3 to 5 minutes.

In another bowl, whisk together flour,
baking soda, ginger, cinnamon, cloves, and
salt. Slowly add dry mixture into butter and
brown sugar mixture and beat for 1 minute.

Add 1 egg at a time, beating well after each
addition. Beat in molasses. Heat apple juice
in microwave until hot and add to mixture;
beat until batter is smooth and creamy.

Pour batter into prepared pan and bake for
about 30 to 35 minutes.

Remove from oven and carefully take ginger-bread from pan by grabbing the extended foil edges to pull the entire piece out at one time. Cool on rack on foil for 15 minutes. Remove from rack to a flat surface and cut into 2-inch-square pieces. Serve warm or at room temperature.

Perfect with a cup of tea!

Little Lady Fruit Sandwiches

Let's get decorating!

1 recipe Gingerbread Tea
  Loaves (see page 50)*

1 (8-ounce) container
  soft-spread cream cheese
  or mascarpone

1 tablespoon honey

1 teaspoon cinnamon

Pink paste food coloring

1 kiwi, peeled, quartered, and
  thinly sliced

½ cup blueberries

½ cup raspberries

2 bananas, peeled, halved
  lengthwise, and thinly sliced

1 nectarine, thinly sliced

6 to 8 strawberries, thinly sliced

Slice the gingerbread into 2-inch squares
and then cut the squares in half horizontally.
Set aside.

Place cream cheese or mascarpone in a
small mixing bowl and add honey and
cinnamon. Stir with a spatula to blend.
Add food coloring and stir to mix in color.

Spread gingerbread squares on top with
the mixture. Decorate with your choice
of fruits and serve.

*This recipe only uses about half of the
gingerbread.*

A fruity favorite
finger food!

Makes 24

Bitsy Bacon and Cheese Rolls

Let's get rolling!

1 (8-count) can refrigerated crescent rolls

6 slices bacon, chopped, cooked, and drained

1 cup grated mozzarella or Swiss cheese

Makes 16 rolls

Itsy–bitsy bites!

Preheat oven to 375 degrees F. Line a cookie sheet with foil and spray with nonstick cooking spray.

Remove crescent rolls from container and lay on a flat surface that has been lightly dusted with flour. Turn over each crescent roll to coat both sides with flour.

Cut each crescent roll in half lengthwise to make two long, thin triangles.

Place approximately ½ teaspoon bacon bits and ½ teaspoon grated cheese on the widest portion of each triangle. Roll up each crescent roll jellyroll style, starting at the widest end. Place rolls seam side down on prepared cookie sheet about 1 inch apart.

Bake for 10 to 12 minutes, or until golden brown. Remove from oven. Cool 5 minutes on pan and serve.

Rainbow-Colored Eggs

Let's get mixing!

6 hard-boiled eggs, peeled and
   sliced in half horizontally

3 tablespoons finely chopped
   celery

3 tablespoons finely grated
   carrots

3 tablespoons mayonnaise or
   plain yogurt

1 teaspoon honey mustard

1 teaspoon dill pickle juice

Salt and pepper to taste

Assorted liquid food coloring

Makes 12

Treasure-filled
little treats!

Set aside several small plastic ziplock bags. Carefully remove cooked egg yolks from eggs and place in a mixing bowl. Set the hollowed out eggs covered in the refrigerator until ready to fill.

Add celery, carrots, mayonnaise or yogurt, honey mustard, pickle juice, salt, and pepper to the yolks. Stir well to combine all ingredients.

Divide yolk mixture equally between three small bowls and add 1 to 2 drops food coloring to each bowl. Stir to incorporate colors into egg yolks.

Scoop equal amounts of yolk mixture into plastic bags and carefully seal shut. Snip the end off one corner of each bag with a pair of scissors and squirt the mixture evenly into the hollowed-out eggs. Place eggs in refrigerator, covered, until ready to serve.

Pink-and-White Star Bites

Let's get baking!

1 (8-count) can refrigerator
   biscuits

8 small slices mozzarella
   cheese

8 small slices deli ham

1 tablespoon mustard

Makes 8 bites

Preheat oven to 350 degrees F. Line a cookie sheet with foil and spray with nonstick cooking spray.

Remove biscuits from can and place onto a floured surface. Turn biscuits to coat each side lightly with flour. Cut each biscuit into a star shape with a small cookie cutter.

Use a slightly smaller cookie cutter to cut cheese and ham into star shapes. Spread each biscuit with mustard and top with cheese and ham stars.

Place on prepared cookie sheet and bake for 10 to 12 minutes, or until bottom edges are lightly browned. Remove from oven and let cool on pan for 5 minutes. Serve warm or at room temperature.

The "star" of your party!

Jeweled Crown Biscuits

Let's get baking!

8 pieces flatbread

8 slices American cheese

1 each red, yellow, orange, and green bell peppers

Makes 8

Preheat oven to 350 degrees F. Line a cookie sheet with foil and spray with nonstick cooking spray. Set aside.

Cut each flatbread with a large crown-shaped cookie cutter. Cut cheese into various sizes and shapes. Using small cookie cutters or a sharp knife, cut bell peppers into various sizes and shapes.

Put each flatbread crown on the prepared cookie sheet and decorate with the cheese and bell peppers to resemble different shapes and sizes of colored jewels. Bake for 5 to 7 minutes, until cheese has softened and melted slightly. Remove from oven, cool on pan for 1 minute, and then place on a serving tray.

A crowning achievement!

Fairy Princess Fruity Toast

Let's get toasting!

Preheat oven to 350 degrees F. Line a cookie sheet with foil.

Remove crusts from bread and cut bread into assorted shapes with cookie cutters. Place bread cutouts on prepared cookie sheet and bake for 5 to 7 minutes, or until edges are very lightly browned. Remove pan from oven and lift sheet of foil with bread from pan onto your work area.

Spread each toast with Nutella and top with 2 to 3 strawberry slices. Transfer to a serving platter and garnish with mint sprigs.

12 slices whole wheat bread

½ to ¾ cup Nutella

1 cup thinly sliced strawberries

Mint sprigs for garnish

Fruity toast to share with a friend!

Makes 12-24

Chicken Salad Sushi Rolls

Let's get rolling!

6 (6- to 8-inch) whole wheat
  or veggie tortillas

1 cup cooked brown or white
  rice, cooled

1 purchased rotisserie
  chicken, sliced into thin
  strips, skin removed

1 cup matchstick sliced carrots

1 cup matchstick sliced and
  peeled apples

6 to 8 plum or cherry
  tomatoes, finely chopped

Makes about 30

It's sushi time!

Lay out 6 tortillas. Spread equal amounts of rice onto each tortilla, spreading the rice almost to the edge of the tortilla.

Place 2 to 3 chicken strips about 1 inch off center on each tortilla. Place 2 to 4 sliced carrots and apples on top of the chicken.

Begin to roll up each tortilla starting on the side closest to the chicken. Make the roll as tight as possible. Continue until all tortillas are securely wrapped. Wrap each rolled tortilla in foil or waxed paper. Place them on a cookie sheet and refrigerate for at least 30 minutes, or up to 4 hours.

Take rolls from refrigerator and remove foil or waxed paper. With a serrated knife, cut each roll into 5 "sushi slices." Top each slice with chopped tomatoes, grated carrots, or tiny slivers of apple.

Collect them all!

www.gibbs-smith.com

www.batterupkids.com

www.kidscookingshop.com